BLOSSOM   'T

New and quicker ways to make su$ using blossom and calyx cutters

Margaret Ford

|CelCakes|

© Copyright Margaret Ford 1992 Reprinted May 1994
Published by CelCakes, Gate Helmsley, York.
ISBN 1 872896 03 0
Photography Chris Mason
Artwork by Maxiprint
Designed and printed by Maxiprint, Colour Printers, York

CONTENTS

Introduction	3
Basic Techniques & Equipment	
Using the CelPad	4
Blossom & Calyx cutters	6
Flowers Formers	7
Roses	
Roses	8
The Calyx & Leaves	11
Full Blown Roses	13
Christmas Rose	15
Carnations & Sweet Peas	
Quick Carnations	16
'One piece' Sweet Peas	18
Azaleas	
'One piece' Azaleas	21
Narrow petal Azalea	23
Pansies & Anemones	
Pansies	24
Anemones	27
Lilies	
Quick 'one piece' Lily	30
Longiflora Lily	31
Orchids	
Quick Cymbidium Orchid	32
Cattleya Orchid	33
More flowers to try	
Daffodil	35
Tulip	36
Cyclamen	38
Arranging flowers	
Using CelPots	39
Natural settings	40
Bouquet setting	41
Triangular settings	42
Specimen and Posy settings	44
Templates etc.	
Cutter and leaf templates	46
Flower paste recipe and gum	47
The author	48

INTRODUCTION

So many people have asked me to produce a booklet with full details on making roses that I felt I must do it, and here it is! Though you may have developed your own method for roses, the added detail in this booklet may introduce some new techniques and tips to enhance your own preferred method. In the same way as making roses by adding several petals at once, it is possible to make many other flowers from blossom and calyx cutters, often significantly reducing the working time! As a result, I have included several other 'blossom cutter' flowers as well.

Perhaps the most widely used sugar flowers in cake decoration are roses, carnations and sweet peas and they can all be made from the blossom cutter. The carnations are more realistic and the sweet peas are so much easier, (with practice).

Sugar flowers can be made to look extremely lifelike - almost indistinguishable from the real thing - but this does take a lot of time. Making flowers for a competition where near perfection is required, is a different task to trying to achieve a realistic effect which takes much less working time. I have extended the usual blossom cutter range by introducing six-petalled blossoms as well as the accompanying six-pointed calyx. With these additional cutters, more flowers are possible - and the methods represent such a saving in time. It is possible to make lilies and orchids within a few minutes.

I hope you enjoy trying out the new techniques, and that you will be encouraged to try out even more flowes than the ones covered in this booklet. We need to allow our cutters and our imagination to realise their full potential. After all, we are all original in our approach to sugarcraft and that is what makes our treasured hobby (or business) thrive. We must never think that a certain way is the only way - it is one way, but there will be others. We should never feel that we all have to do the same things and always agree on methods. Remember that "points of conflict can be points of growth" and out of our differences, new concepts and ideas can grow and "blossom".

Enjoy the experience of blossoming out!

Margaret Ford

BASIC TECHNIQUES AND EQUIPMENT

(1) USING THE CELPAD

The CelPad is now recognised by thousands as an essential piece of sugarcraft equipment. It eases the thinning of petal edges; it creates an ideal surface for frilling; it allows the distortion of petal shapes to create new profiles and it overcomes the difficulty of paste sticking to warm hands. The special firm foam surface has sufficient flexibility to allow the paste to be worked but yet is not so soft that it results in the paste tearing. Some of the basic uses are covered in the *Blooming Quick* booklet but the following notes should give further indications as to better usage.

Thinning the paste

For stretching and thinning paste, hold the CelStick almost flat to the foam surface and draw firmly over the paste, moving away from the flower centre along a curved path. Pressure is applied on the side of the flexible stick, which will bend, but it will not be damaged. If too much pressure is applied on the end of the stick, it is likely that the paste will tear. To thin the petal edges however, you should hold the CelStick (or larger CelPin, or balling tool) in an upright position (similar to holding a pencil) and just roll along the petal edge.

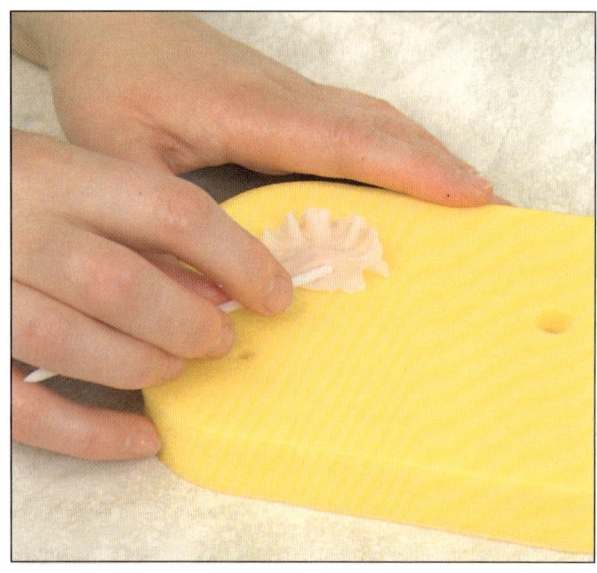

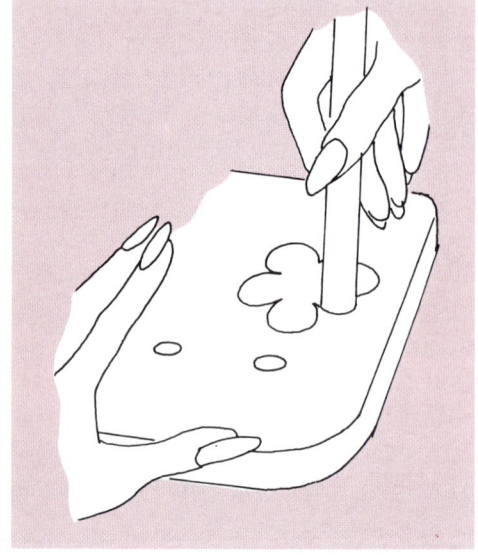

Changing the shape of petals:

(a) To broaden and lengthen petals

Petal shapes may be changed once cut out with a cutter. When laid on the CelPad they can be broadened or lengthened by working with modelling tools, CelSticks, CelPins and balling tools. To broaden a petal, roll the paste from side to side, whilst pressing firmly against the foam surface. To lengthen a petal, roll the paste lengthways along the petal, again applying some pressure.

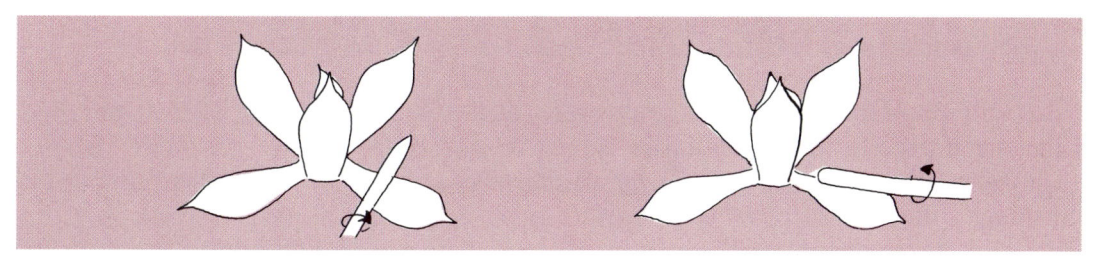

(b) To create a different outline
In a similar way to thinning petals, it is possible to stretch or push the paste to give it a different outline shape. To create a pointed petal from a rounded cutter shape, for example, simply stroke the rounded end of the modelling tool along one side and off at the centre, and then repeat on the other side. The result will be a petal that is drawn to a point.

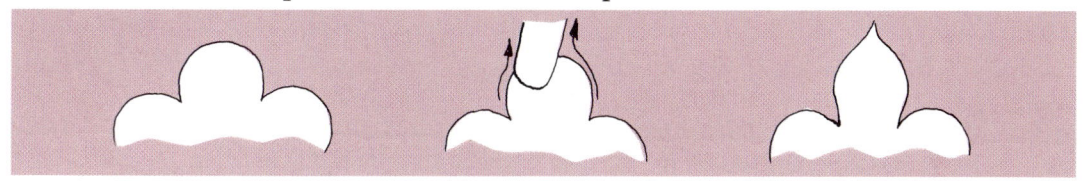

(c) To combine petals
If two petals are overlapped slightly, laid on the CelPad and then rubbed over the front and back join, with a rounded end of a CelPin or balling tool, the paste will become fused together and will resemble a larger petal. This can be very useful where a flower might have four petals of a similar size and one petal which is larger (e.g. sweet pea or pansy).

Mexican Hats
"Mexican hats" can be made quickly by using the coated side of the CelPad. Grease round the selected hole with white fat (or shortening) and press a ball of paste over the hole and then roll flat with a modelling tool. Some paste will have been pushed down the hole to make the stem. If a disc of paste is used instead of a ball, the stem is shorter. The size of hole used will alter the width of the stem.

Veining
If the pointed end of the CelStick is used to work the paste it will leave quick basic "vein" markings as it thins. However, it is important to avoid too much pressure so that the paste is not torn away. With practice, veining can be achieved very quickly in this way. When the CelStick point is drawn over the edge of the paste it gives a slightly jagged effect, which can be very useful when making leaves without serrated cutters. Both petal and leaf veins can be made with veining tools or petal and leaf veiners (more realistic).

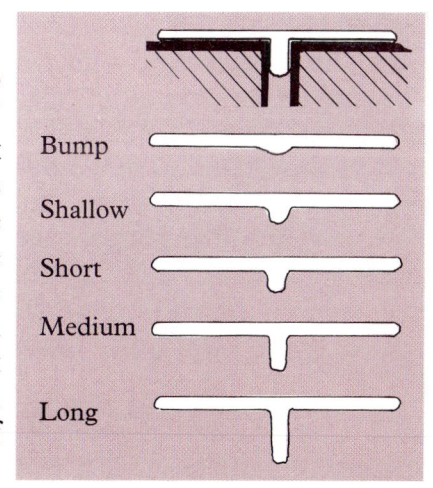

Bump
Shallow
Short
Medium
Long

(2) BLOSSOM AND CALYX CUTTERS

You will probably be well acquainted with the wide range of five-petalled blossom cutters that are available. Made from either metal or moulded plastic, they vary in size from very tiny plunger blossoms to the large 3" cutter. Similarly, there are many five-pointed calyx cutters. The larger sized blossom cutters have enjoyed much popularity in recent years for making quick roses (adding several petals at once, rather than the traditional method of one petal at a time), and you will see my method covered fully in this booklet. Additionally I will be using six petalled blossom cutters and a range of calyx cutters. Some general hints and tips are included here for reference.

TIPS FOR USING BLOSSOM AND CALYX CUTTERS

- Snipping between petals allows more petal separation
- Thinning the petal edges may distort the shape, but give a more natural appearance, just as cupping gives natural curves and is more realistic
- Some flowers have only four petals, and by snipping and removing one, this type of flower is easily created using a five-petalled cutter.
- Narrow pointed leaves can be made with calyx cutters - a six-pointed calyx can be the basis for three pairs of leaves (see carnation).
- Some special leaves (e.g. clover) can be made by using only part of blossom cutter - roll out the paste as usual, with thicker central core and cut out three lobes. Snip between leaves and trim away any excess. Insert a hooked wire, vein and thin edges. Moisten centre with gum and bring side leaves to centre, so that the wire comes from behind the leaves.
- Many calyx cutters have fairly wide sepals. Where a very fine calyx is required (e.g. wild flowers or miniature roses), cut out with a calyx cutter and then cut in half - each half will have 2½ points. Split the two large ones into two and re-shape on the CelPad before adding to your flower as a mini-calyx.

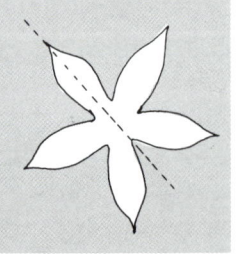

(3) FOAM FORMERS

It is a relatively simple task to make up special formers by clipping and snipping foam pieces. It is possible to make very useful formers to support the one-piece flowers and some examples are shown below. The size of the foam former depends upon the size of flowers being made (and the size of cutter being used), but the general shape is the same:

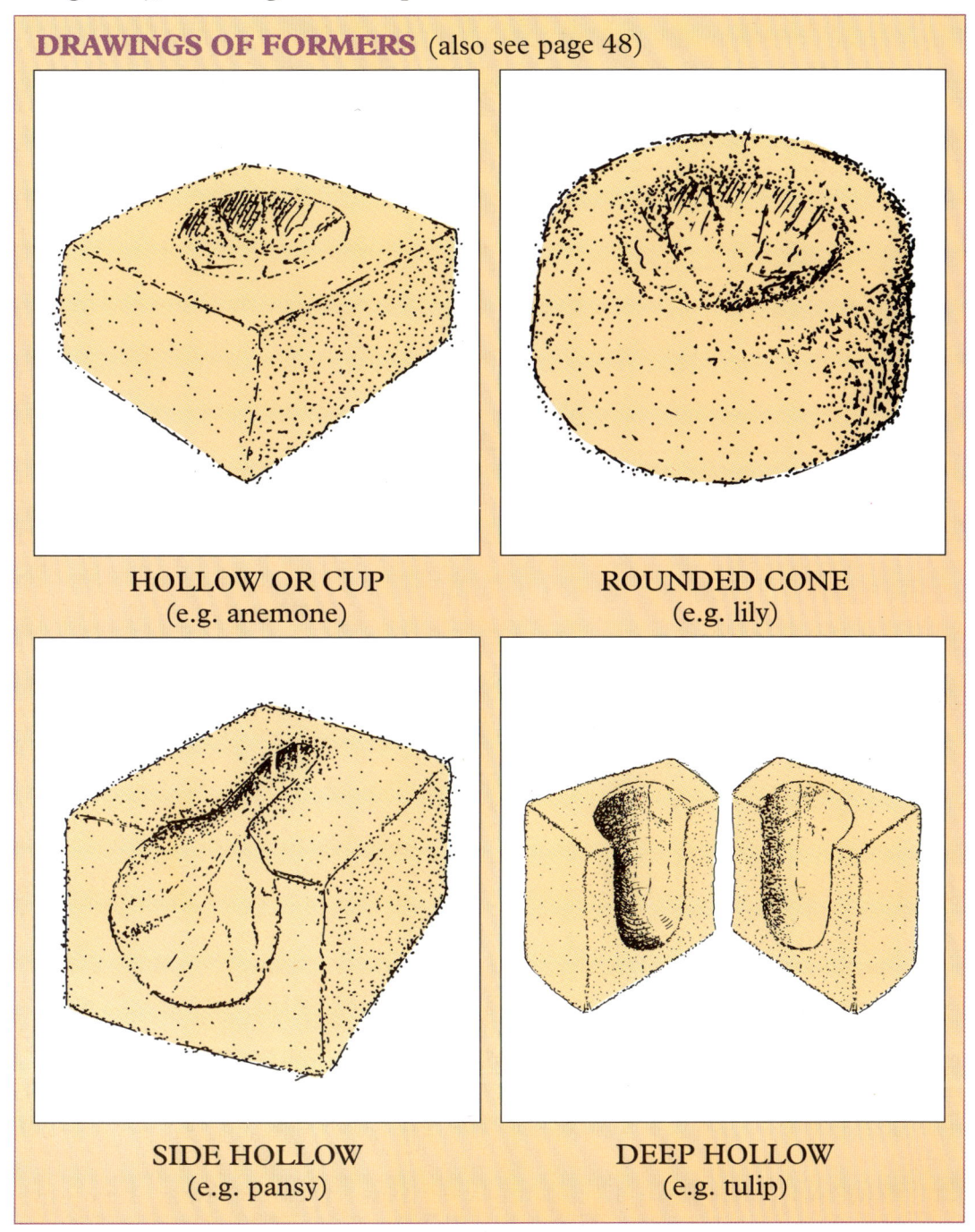

DRAWINGS OF FORMERS (also see page 48)

HOLLOW OR CUP
(e.g. anemone)

ROUNDED CONE
(e.g. lily)

SIDE HOLLOW
(e.g. pansy)

DEEP HOLLOW
(e.g. tulip)

PASTE AND GUM
For notes on flower modelling paste and gum, see page 47

ROSES

The cone size

Take a piece of 28g or 30g florist's wire and bend a small right-angled hook on one end. Hook over the five-petalled cutter and measure across the widest part. This will give the required length of wire to be looped and twisted together into a cone shape as shown below. The wire loop is then a suitable pattern for the cone size required for the particular cutter being used.

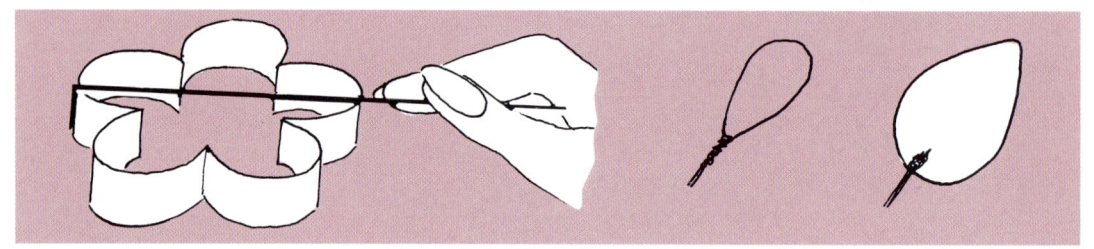

Making the cone

Make an open hook on the end of a 24g wire and dip in gum before pressing into a suitably sized ball of flower paste. Firm round the base with one hand and roll between thumb and fore finger of the other hand at the top end, to give the desired pointed cone shape. Check for size with wire pattern and reduce/increase if required. Allow to dry until quite hard.

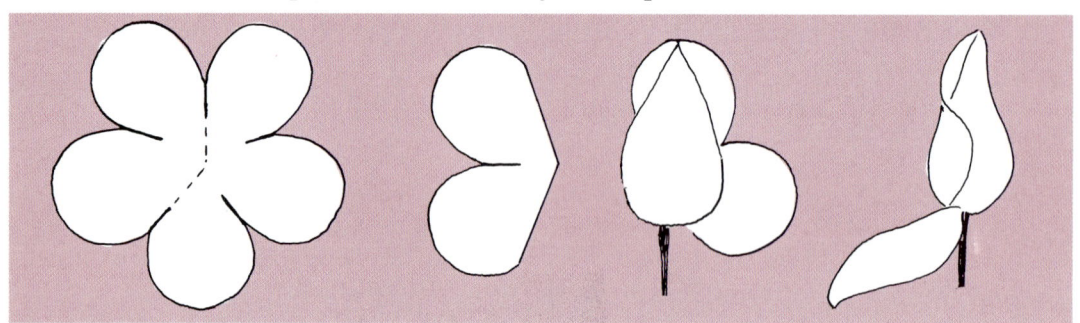

The inner petals

Roll out flower paste very thinly and cut out with blossom cutter - you may find it easier to lay paste over large cutters and roll gently with rolling pin to obtain a cleaner cut. Rub the cutter and paste over the palm of one hand to remove any feathering, before peeling the paste from the cutter. (You will save time at this stage if you cut out several petal layers and place under a plastic flap to prevent drying out - otherwise only cut out what you can use straight away.)

Cut away two petals from a blossom layer (cover the remaining three until required) and snip between. Using a ball tool, or modelling stick, thin the petal edges and cup the two petals. Moisten the surface lightly with gum and lay a dried cone in the centre of one petal. Enclose the cone top tightly within the paste and bring the second petal from the other side and close round to cover. The cone should not be visible from the top.

9

Snip between, thin and cup the other three petals, brush with gum and lay the cone in the centre of one of the end petals. Wrap and overlap the second petal over the first, then the third over the second to evenly distribute the petals.

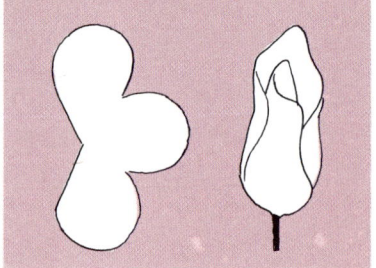

The middle petals

Taking a second layer of petals, snip between the petals, thin and cup as before and gum part way up each petal. Insert the wire down through the centre of the paste, and make sure that the centre of a petal covers the edge of a petal in the previous layer. Now, bring up each petal in turn, overlapping the one before it. Adjust for position and curl edges back to give a natural appearance.

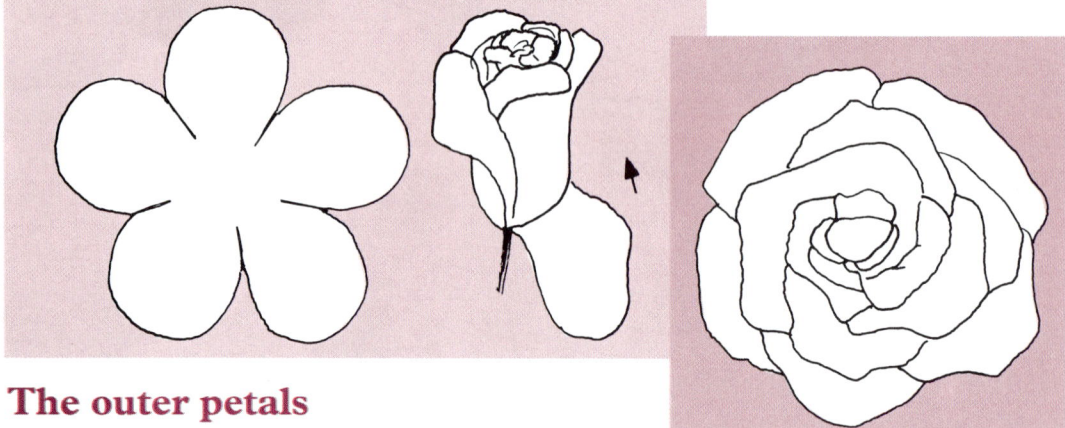

The outer petals

Repeat the last stage with another petal layer, but the blossom shape should be increased in size by rolling gently before snipping between the petals. Add to rose as before, but remember to gum less of the petals since they will need to curl away from previous layers as the flower opens. You may also wish to repeat again with a fourth cutting of petals.

NOTES:

(1) For a bud, only the inner layers would be required, and only up to the middle layer for a part opened flower. For a full flower, more outer layers can be added, but when a larger flower is required, start with a larger blossom cutter to achieve the finished flower more quickly. For a really large flower, start with a really large cutter!

(2) The above method is deliberately quick and simple and should always be used as a starting point for those not familiar with the method. A refinement, which produces an even better looking flower, is to bring up the petals in the order shown rather than just working round in sequence.

ROSE LEAVES

Rose leaves are made in the usual way using special leaf cutters, but where tiny leaves are required, the method described in the general notes could be used. When colouring rose leaves, a combination of greens, browns and reds will give a realistic looking leaf finish. If a dark shade is required (e.g. dark green), add a little black to the powder mixture.

When assembling flowers with leaves, individual leaves can be added to the arrangement. For a more natural or specimen flower, the leaves should be grouped in threes, fives or sevens, with the largest leaf at the top.

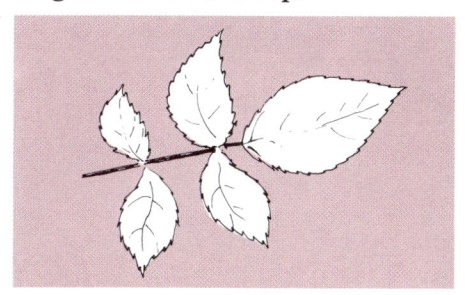

GENERAL NOTES

(1) Leaves are made by rolling out green paste thinly from the centre to each side, leaving a ridge in the middle, where a fine gummed and hooked wire can be inserted.

(2) Leaves can be shaped with cutters or by using a template or even freehand. The serrated edges can be created by laying the cut leaf on a pad or rolling board and drawing a pointed modelling stick or veiner tool firmly over the edge of the paste at intervals along the length.

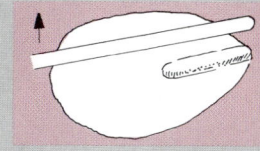

(3) When making leaves, the paste should not be too dark in colour. After drying, the more natural shadings can be achieved by brushing on powder colourings, giving the leaf more variation and depth of colour.

(4) If the coloured leaf is passed through steam (e.g. from a kettle), the colours will blend.

(5) Gently brushing the finished leaf with white fat (softened veg. fat or shortening) gives a natural sheen. Only rarely should confectioner's glaze be used, as this tends to give too high a gloss finish except for leaves like holly.

THE CALYX

The rose calyx is usually lighter on the inside and this feature can be achieved by rolling and cutting the paste in two colours (e.g. flatten a small ball of white paste and place over a similar piece of green paste). For a quick method, lighten the inside of the calyx (or the upper side before attaching to the flower) by dusting with white or white lustre colour.

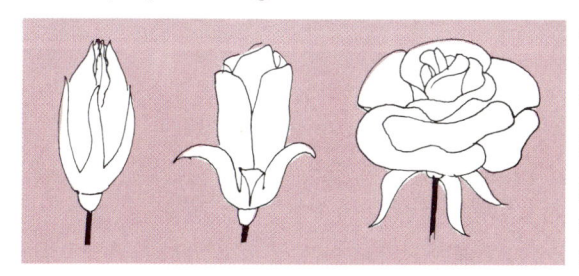

After cutting out with a calyx cutter, the sepal edges may be snipped to give a spiked appearance. When making quick flowers or wiring into sprays, it is best to avoid such fragile details.

The bud calyx is positioned close to the flower, the calyx on the opening flower is seen beginning to turn back, and as the flower opens more fully, the calyx curls well back towards the flower stem.

12

FULL BLOWN ROSE

Flower centre
Wind yellow cotton round finger up to 60 times and insert a 28g or 30g wire through loop and twist and tape tightly. Add a 24g wire and tape the two wires firmly together. Make sure to firmly tape the base of the loop so that the cottons become bunched together. Cut the loop and trim stamens to the desired length (approx. ⅓ length of petal). The ends of the cotton can be brushed with gum and dipped into either yellow textured colouring or a mixture of fine semolina or rice flour and colouring.

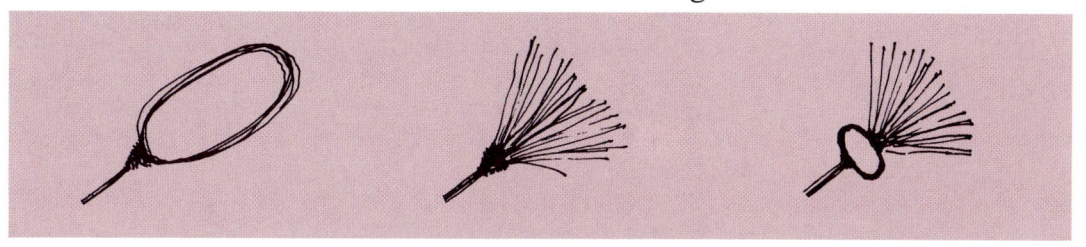

The inner petals
Moisten the base of the stamen centre and attach a small collar of paste, and allow to dry. Be sure to keep the collar fairly shallow so that the petals can be closed around the centre. Use a blossom cutter, and cut petals (several cut-outs can be made at this stage to save time, if they are stored under a plastic flap). Snip between the petals with scissors or a craft knife. "Ball" and "cup" the five petals on the pad surface, using a balling tool. Moisten the centre with gum and also one edge of each petal. Insert the prepared stamen cottons through the middle and form round, overlapping each petal. Leave the cupped petals suspended upside down for a few minutes to dry - when using larger cutters, the petals will need to be left a little longer to dry out and become firm. When drying, the flower must always hang vertically and not to either side, so that the stamen centre remains central to the flower head. Prepare several flowers to this stage.

The middle petals
When the first layer of petals has firmed sufficiently to support the rest of the flower, all the other layers can be added without waiting for them to dry in between. Add a second and a third layer of petals, stretching slightly by rolling lightly before snipping between the petals. Ensure that the layers are added

with petal centres overlapping the petal edges in the previous layer. Hang upside down between layers to hold the flower shape. The petal edges can be curled back over a small modelling stick to give a natural effect. (The size of the petal cut-out will need to be increased slightly, by rolling before snipping between the petals from the third layer onwards).

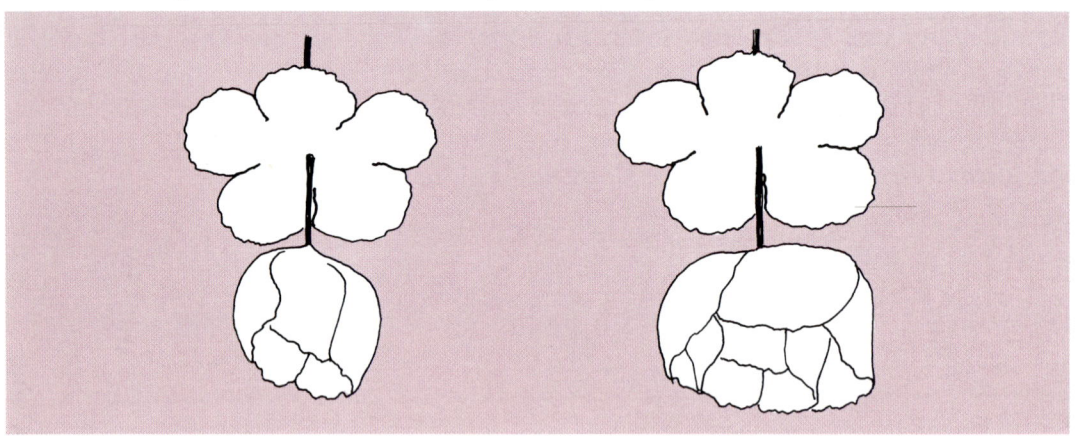

The outer petals

For the fourth and fifth layers, stretch, snip and cup as before and then turn over before attaching to the flower. By reversing, the petals will turn down when added to the flower and give a drooped effect which is more realistic. It is easier to gum the back of the flower for the last two layers than the petals themselves. Curl the edges and leave upside down to dry completely.

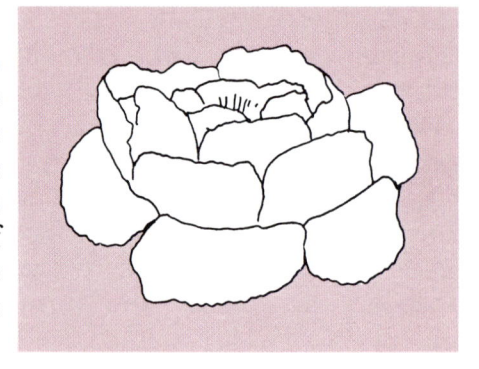

Leaves and calyx

Add leaves and calyx as required - a calyx on this rose is very vulnerable if being wired into a spray. The stem can be strengthened by taping in a 24g wire, if required.

NOTE

(1) On any flowers or leaves, extra wires can be taped on for strength if you find that on completion the stem is not strong enough to give firm support.

(2) In reality, the colour of rose petals can vary considerably both in depth of colour from the centre to the outer petals and as the flower matures. Often the centre of the flower is darker and this effect can be achieved by using darker coloured paste for the central layers. Another method which is very effective is to roll a lighter layer of paste over a darker layer, so that they appear as one, but coloured darker on one side than the other. If the rose is made up always putting the darker colour towards the centre, a very natural looking flower results.

CHRISTMAS ROSE

Flower centre

To make the flower centre, wind yellow cotton round a finger 30-40 times and insert a 28g covered wire through the loop and twist tightly. Tape firmly with florist's tape and trim the "stamens" to the desired length. Moisten the ends and dip into yellow textured colouring to resemble stamen ends. Make a tiny ball in yellow paste and dip in textured colouring. Spread open the cotton centre and brush with gum before pressing the ball of paste into the middle of the stamens to complete the flower centre.

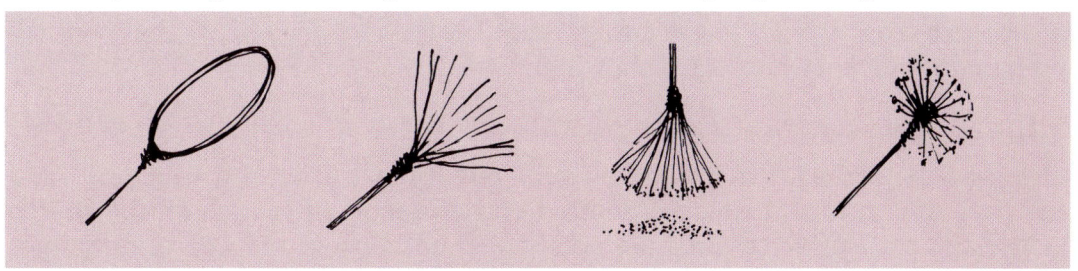

The Petals

Roll out white paste on the lightly greased, coated side of the pad to form a small bump (see page 5). Using a large blossom cutter, cut out the petals, snipping between with scissors or a craft knife. Place on the uncoated side of the pad and thin the petals along each side and then outwards at the centre. This will produce petals that are more pointed in shape.

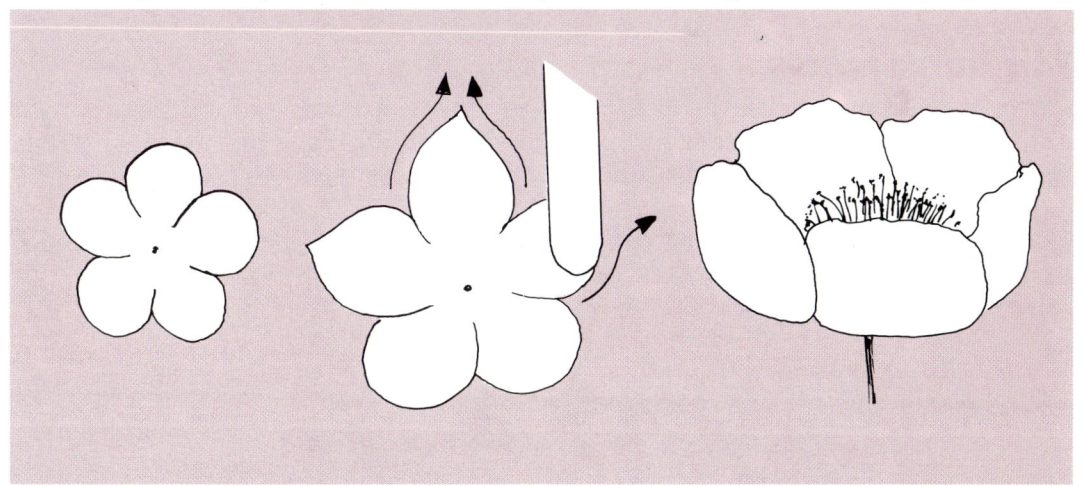

Cup the petals and lightly dust the middle with green dusting powder. Brush with gum before threading the flower centre into position. Allow to dry thoroughly in a cup-shaped former.

Leaves

The Christmas rose does not have a calyx and leaves can be cut freehand (see leaf templates on page 46). The leaves are dark green and shiny.

CARNATIONS

Using a blossom cutter for the carnation results in a more open flower, showing the individual petals as seen in reality.

Flower centre
For the flower centre, push an elongated ball of paste (pea-sized for a 2" cutter) onto the end of a hooked 26g wire. The centres should be prepared in advance and dried thoroughly.

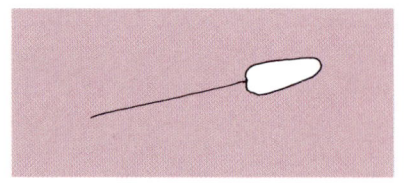

The inner petals
Using a six-petalled blossom cutter, cut out a petal layer and vein, thin and frill each one in turn, using the pointed end of a modelling stick on the coated side of the pad. Work towards the petal edges and ensure that the veining lines all radiate from the centre of the paste. Push the wire down through the centre and bring up three alternate petals and loosely pinch together. In a similar way, bring up the other three petals. Mould the flower back with fingers, but allow it to retain the characteristic bulbous shape.

The outer petals
Cut out another petal layer and vein and frill exactly as before. Brush with gum and push the wire stem through the centre and bring up alternate petals (as before) and pinch together. Re-shape the flower back. Extra layers can be added. Flowers with one, two and three layers should be arranged together to represent flowers at different stages of growth.

The calyx and leaves
Make a calyx from green paste (some carnations have a calyx with five points, some with six) and position the calyx points close to the flower back. The leaves can be cut freehand, but try using a calyx cutter for the small leaves. Cut out green paste with a calyx cutter and cut away two sepals. Thin and stretch on the surface of the pad. These narrow "leaves" can be positioned in pairs on the stem (see page 6).

17

SWEET PEAS

Flower centre
The flower centre is made by placing a small ball of flower paste onto the end of a hooked 26g covered wire. Flatten and allow to dry.

The petals
Using suitably coloured paste and a five-petalled blossom cutter, cut out the sweet pea petals in one piece. Snip down deeply between the petals, slightly overlap two petals and fuse together into one large petal by working on the surface of the pad with a balling tool. Rub over the join back and front until it disappears and finish by gently frilling the outside edge to give a natural effect. Gently frill the edges of the other three petals. Only the lower half of the two side petals. Some varieties are more frilled than others.

Brush a line of gum from the centre of the large petal down to the mid-point of the paste and bringing the un-frilled part of the left hand petal up, rotate into place as shown below. Repeat for the right hand petal and then gum down the centre and flip over and fold back the last small petal.

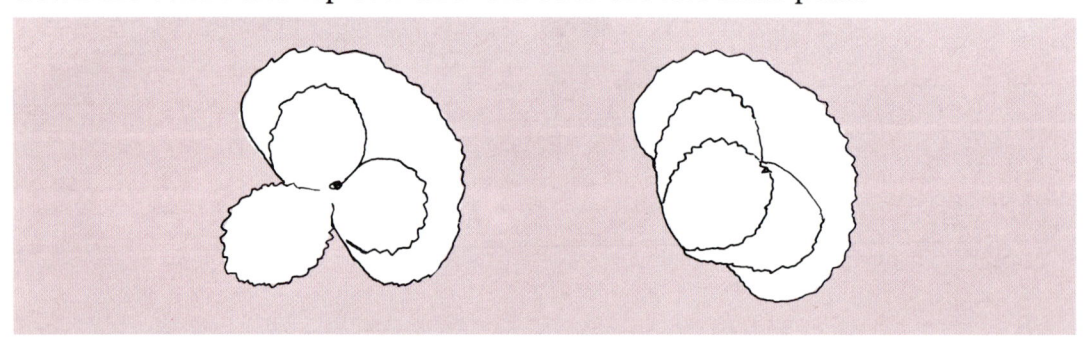

Gum one half of the small central petal, place the dried wired centre (seed pod) in the middle and fold the flower in half. Lightly pinch the back of the flower and pinch the two sides of the seed pod to close. Bring the inner petals forward and arrange the back petal into a suitable shape. Leave to dry and then add a tiny five sepalled calyx.

The buds
Buds are made from only three petals, which are moulded round a dried centre. A tiny five-sepalled calyx is added when the bud is dry. After a light dusting with suitable colouring, the stem is sharply bent down in characteristic fashion.

The leaves and tendrils
Tendrils can be made by curving fine wires. As the flowers are taped together, add the tendrils and tape into the stem. Leaves can be cut freehand, thinned and veined and vary greatly in size - a leaf template can be found on page 47. The leaves are not usually found on the flower stems, but at growth points and on new shots.

NOTES
(1) The sweet pea can also be made using a six-petalled blossom cutter, when three petals are overlapped to form the larger petal. This produces a flower more like the old fashioned sweet pea or the bush sweet pea.

(2) An airbrush can be very effective in colouring sweet peas because it successfully produces vibrant colours and subtle shadings as seen in the real flowers.

20

AZALEAS

There are many varieties, with different petal shapes and colours, but most have five petals. For the broad petalled flower, use a blossom cutter and the narrow petalled flowers, a calyx cutter.

The Stamen centre

To make the flower centre, tape 5 doubled or 10 single stamens and one extra long stamen (the pistil), in matching colour to the flower being made, to a 26g florist's wire. The stamens and pistil should curve upwards - bend and curl over a small brush handle.

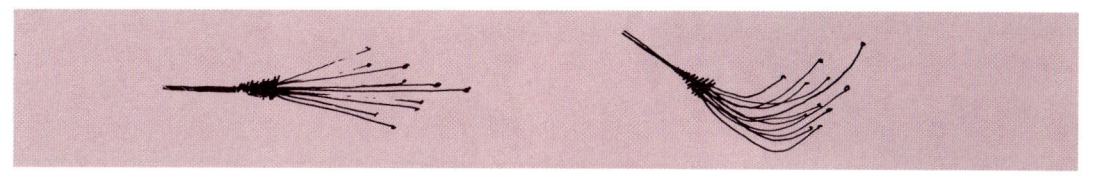

The petals

Using coloured paste, make a disc and roll out over the middle-sized hole in pad (lightly greased and on the coated side) so that a "bump" is created (see notes on page 5). Turn over onto a board and cut out a ring of petals with a five-petalled blossom cutter. Snip down between the petals and invert back into the hole in the pad (foam surface). Encourage the petals into a more pointed shape by rolling on the edges and off at the centre (see notes on page 5, or similar to method for Christmas rose). Thin and soften the petal edges and vein with a modelling stick or petal veiner.

Brush gum on the stamen centre, thread down through the petals and pinch onto the wire at the back. Place in a foam former (shallow hollow), and arrange petals as illustrated into a natural setting. The order of the petals is important and the back petal overlaps those to each side, which in turn overlap the front petals. The left front petal should overlap the right one.

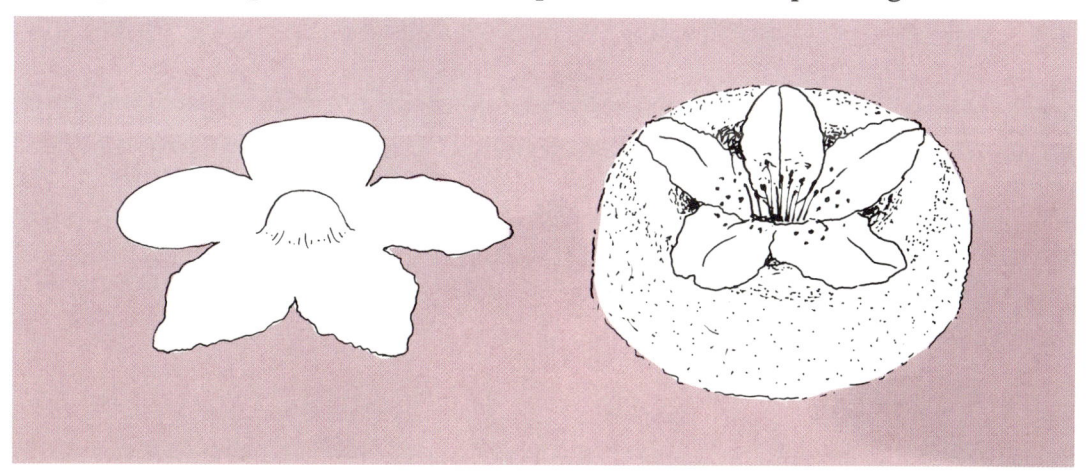

22

Flower colouring

When thoroughly dry, dust with colouring along the central veins and add a little green colouring at the base and back of the flower head where it joins the wire. The characteristic azalea spots are seen on the back and side petals, but not on the lower front petals. Not all azaleas have spots on the petals.

The leaves

A template for the azalea leaves can be found on page 46, but size depends very much upon the variety being made. Some have relatively large dark green leaves, and others have narrower light green leaves. The leaves should not be rolled too thin. After dusting with colour, gloss by brushing with white fat.

Check carefully on the petal shape with the real flower or a good book.
- Some petals are broad and rounded and some are broad but more pointed, so the paste will need to be reshaped.
- Some varieties have smooth petals, whilst others have very frilled petal edges.
- Some varieties have very thin pointed petals, where a calyx cutter would be more appropriate to use than a blossom cutter - see photograph below
- Azalea flowers can have more than five petals - some hybrids may have up to seven.

PANSY

The flower stem

Prepare the wire stem by taping tightly five times round the end of a suitable wire (gauge will depend upon cutter size; e.g. 28g for 1½" cutter) with third width white florist's tape about ⅓" along the wire. Bend as shown (120°) ¼" from the end.

The petals

Make a medium mexican hat by rolling a ball of paste thinly over the smallest hole on the lightly greased, coated side of the pad. Remove and place on a board and cut out petals using a 1½" six-petalled blossom cutter. Snip between petals fairly deeply, except between petals 4 and 5.

Slightly overlap petals 1 and 2 and fuse together by rolling on both sides on the foam surface of the pad. Turn over and place stem in a hole and then thin and vein all petals - pressing petals against a veiner gives a very realistic effect, but, as with making all flowers with multi-petalled cutters, take care to have the veins running from the flower centre and not across the petals.

Assembly of the flower

Dip the end of the prepared bent wire into gum and push through the flower centre at an angle, so that the wire comes through above the spur at the back (as shown on the next page).

Pinch the flower at the sides and place in a foam former. Arrange the petals so that the back ones overlap (sometimes left over right and sometimes right over left). When completely dry, dust in suitable colours and bend wire downwards with tweezers.

SPUR

Calyx, leaves and buds

The calyx can be made by rolling out green paste over the smallest hole in the pad to give a fine mexican hat. Cut out with a small calyx cutter and snip to the centre between two sepals. Open out flat and thin the sepals at the top and bottom to give tiny spurs on each. Gum and attach to the back of the flower with the central sepal behind the overlap of the top two petals of the flower.

Buds can be made by attaching a small piece of green paste to the end of a hooked 28g wire. Surround the paste with a calyx and bend the wire stem down. Opening buds can be made using three petals pinched together, with a calyx added.

The leaves vary a great deal in size and some shape templates are given on page 47. They should be assembled in groups of varying size and shape with a suitable selection of buds, partly opened and fully opened flowers.

An airbrush can be particularly effective in colouring the pansy, because it allows some of the very rich velvety colouring effects to be produced - finish off by dusting with a little powder colouring to give subtle tints and fine detail.

26

ANEMONES

There are many varieties of anemone. Though some have five petals, others have six or many more in single or multiple layers. The flowers are characteristically very strongly coloured.

The flower centre

To make the flower centre, place a small ball of paste on the end of a 26g wire (for flower made with 2" cutter) and dip into black textured colouring (or coloured semolina). Take some white cotton and wind round a finger about 30 times. Thread a 28g wire through and twist tightly. Bind firmly with florist's tape and then cut the loops to make the stamens. After trimming to size, curve and dust with black dusting powder and then moisten the end with gum. Dip into black textured colouring to achieve the effect of stamen ends. Place the prepared centre down through the cotton stamens and bind both wires together.

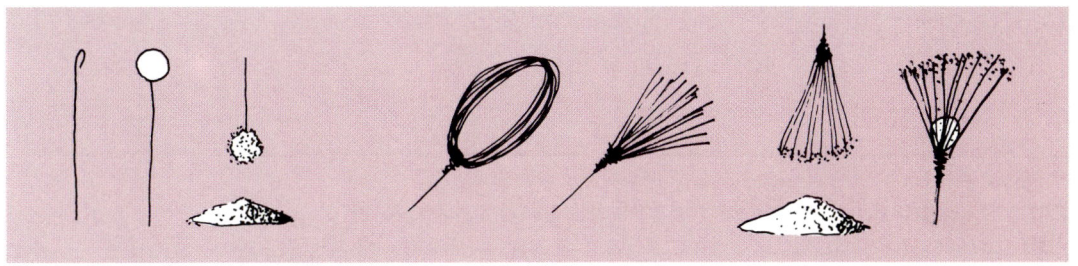

The petals

Roll out some coloured flower paste and cut out a layer of petals, using a six-petalled blossom cutter. Snip between the petals and thin edges and cup as required. The petals generally do not have frilled edges. Whilst the paste is still soft, paint on white markings around the centre of the petals, using a soft brush with water and white powder colouring.

Flower assembly

Soften a small amount of paste with gum and use this to secure the petals to the cotton centre. Push the flower centre down through the middle of the painted petals and place in a cupped former (e.g., apple carton or snipped foam) to hold the flower in the characteristic shape. Leave to dry, and then dust as required.

The leaves

Roll out some paste as for wired leaves, leaving a thicker area for the wire. Place a five-petalled blossom cutter over and cut out three petals in paste.

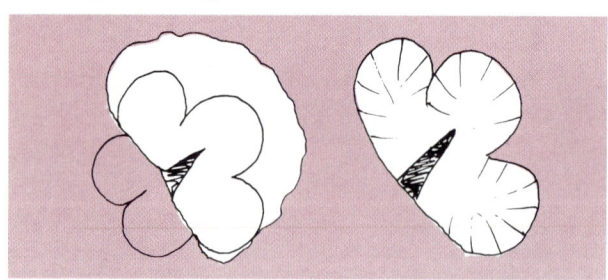

Slash the three 'leaves' with a craft knife as shown and lay on the foam pad surface and stretch, thin and curve the fronds to give a ragged effect. A group of tiny leaves should be placed a short distance from the back of the flower, and larger leaves further down the stem. The anemone does not have a calyx.

> Some varieties do not have black centres - the white flowers often have a green centre with green stamens, and some varieties have double rows of petals. For the double flowers, add another layer of petals.

29

LILIES

The colour of the pistil and stamens depends upon the colour of the finished flower and it is best to work from a real sample or a book illustration.

The flower centre

For the flower centre, cover one stamen (or a very fine wire - 33g) with paste and roll thinly to make the pistil. Pinch the end into three tiny lobes and dip the moistened ends of three pointed stamens in textured colouring. Bend the stamens in half and tape, with the pistil, onto a 26g wire. For larger flowers, use longer stamens and stronger wire.

The flower

Take a disc of paste and roll out over the large hole in the pad to form a short mexican hat - do not roll the paste too thinly. Cut out the petals using a six-pointed calyx cutter, trim the tips as required (some lily petals are more pointed than others), and stretch, shape and thin on the pad. If the petals are thinned alternately more width can be achieved, and when thinning alternate petals, it is possible to move others forward to create space. The first three petals will become the inner petals and should be a little wider than the outer ones. Vein the petals with a petal veiner (or corn husk) and vein down the middle with a veiner tool. To create petals that curve well back, lay the flower head downwards on the foam surface of the pad and draw a modelling tool or balling tool from the petal tips to the flower centre, so that the petals curve upwards.

Flower assembly

Open up the flower centre with a pointed modelling tool. Push and mould the three wider petals to the centre, to become the inner petals, so that the remaining ones make the outer layer. Gum round the stamen centre and insert into the throat of the flower.

Thread the flower centre into place and position in a former - a ring of soft sponge for open lilies (e.g. tiger lily) and a paper cone for longiflora varieties (e.g. Easter lily).

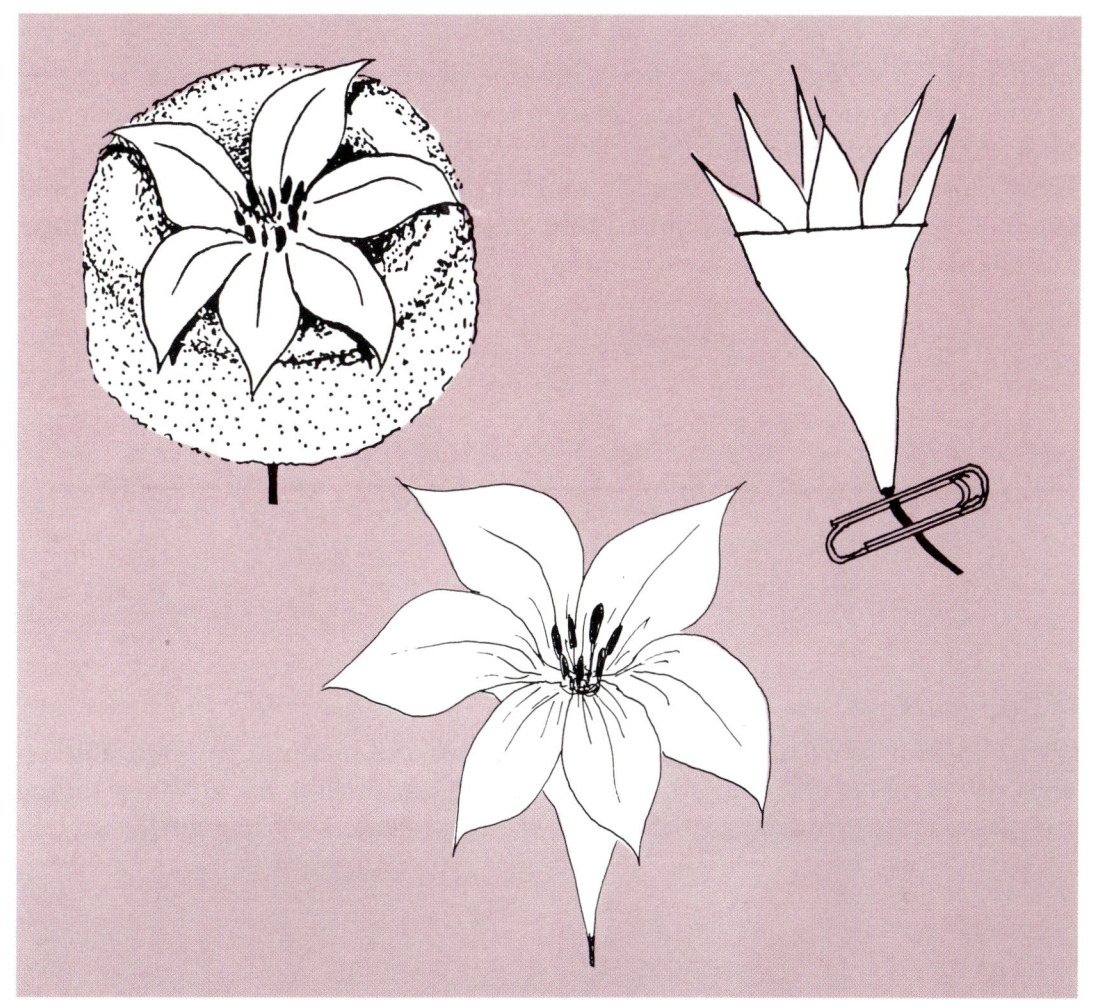

When dry, dust with colouring and add spots as appropriate. There is no calyx, but the base of the flower, should be shaded green where it joins the stem.

NOTES

(1) For the longiflora lily, when rolling out paste on the pad a long back to the mexican hat is required. After thinning the petals, open up this trumpet before adding the stamens.

(2) The pollen head on the stamens of a fully opened lily would split as the flower opens. If desired, this effect can be achieved by adding a small piece of coloured paste to the end of a round headed stamen.

ORCHIDS

Making the column (cymbidium)

Make the column by forming a small piece of paste into a cone. Make a hook on the end of a 24g wire and insert into the narrow end of the cone, securing on the wire by squeezing firmly. Flatten the cone and with a small modelling stick, roll out one side and then the other. Roll out the end to give a "cobra head" shape. Moisten near the top and add a small ball of yellow paste. Split the ball by marking with a pointed tool and then curve over as shown to make the characteristic column. Leave to dry.

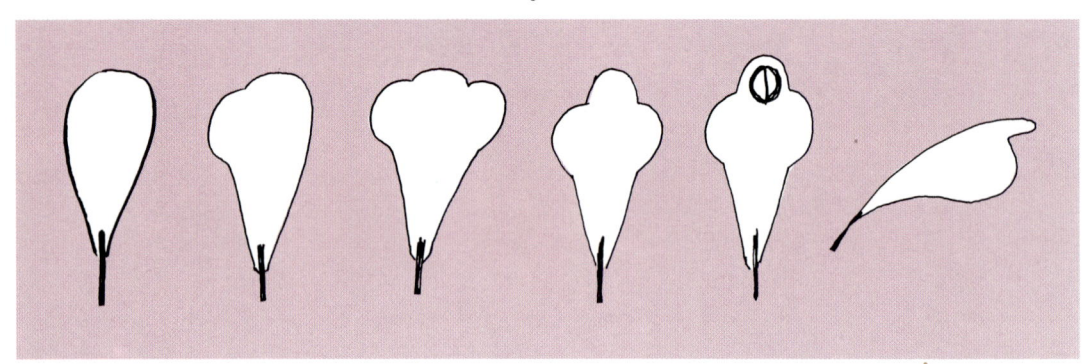

The petals

Flatten a ball of paste into a disc and roll over the medium or large hole on the coated side of the CelPad, to make a medium/shallow back. When rolling out, leave one narrow area thicker than the rest (shaded on diagram).

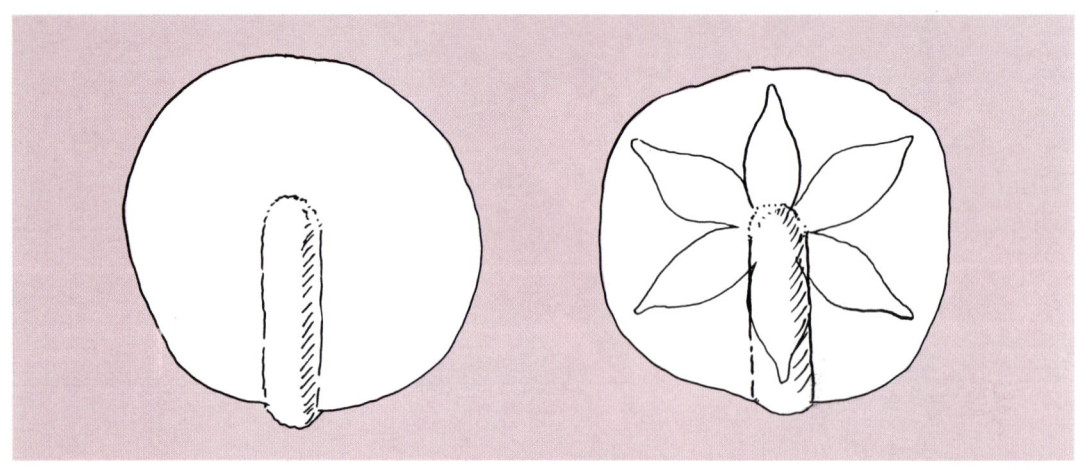

Place a six pointed calyx cutter over the paste and cut out so that one sepal is thicker than the others (this will become the trumpet of the orchid, and the extra paste will allow more scope for stretching and frilling).

Snip towards the centre between each sepal, and cut away the points. Broaden out the top left and top right wing petals by shaping on the uncoated side of the CelPad. Vein with a corn husk or petal veiner. Also work and vein the other petals.

Thin and shape the trumpet (thicker paste) by stretching the paste out at each side and down in the middle. Frill the lower edges of the trumpet.

Flower assembly

When all the petals are formed, moisten the edges of the dry column and push wire down through the centre of the petals. Bring the sides of the trumpet up towards each other and attach to the column. Firm the paste onto the wire at the back and cut away any excess paste. Place in a foam former and support the trumpet with foam chippings. Arrange the petals as required and support as necessary until dry. Colour according to variety of orchid being made.

CATTLEYA ORCHID

To make the cattleya orchid, do not remove the points from the petals but frill the edges of the wing petals. The trumpet should also be frilled more fully than for the cymbidium orchid.

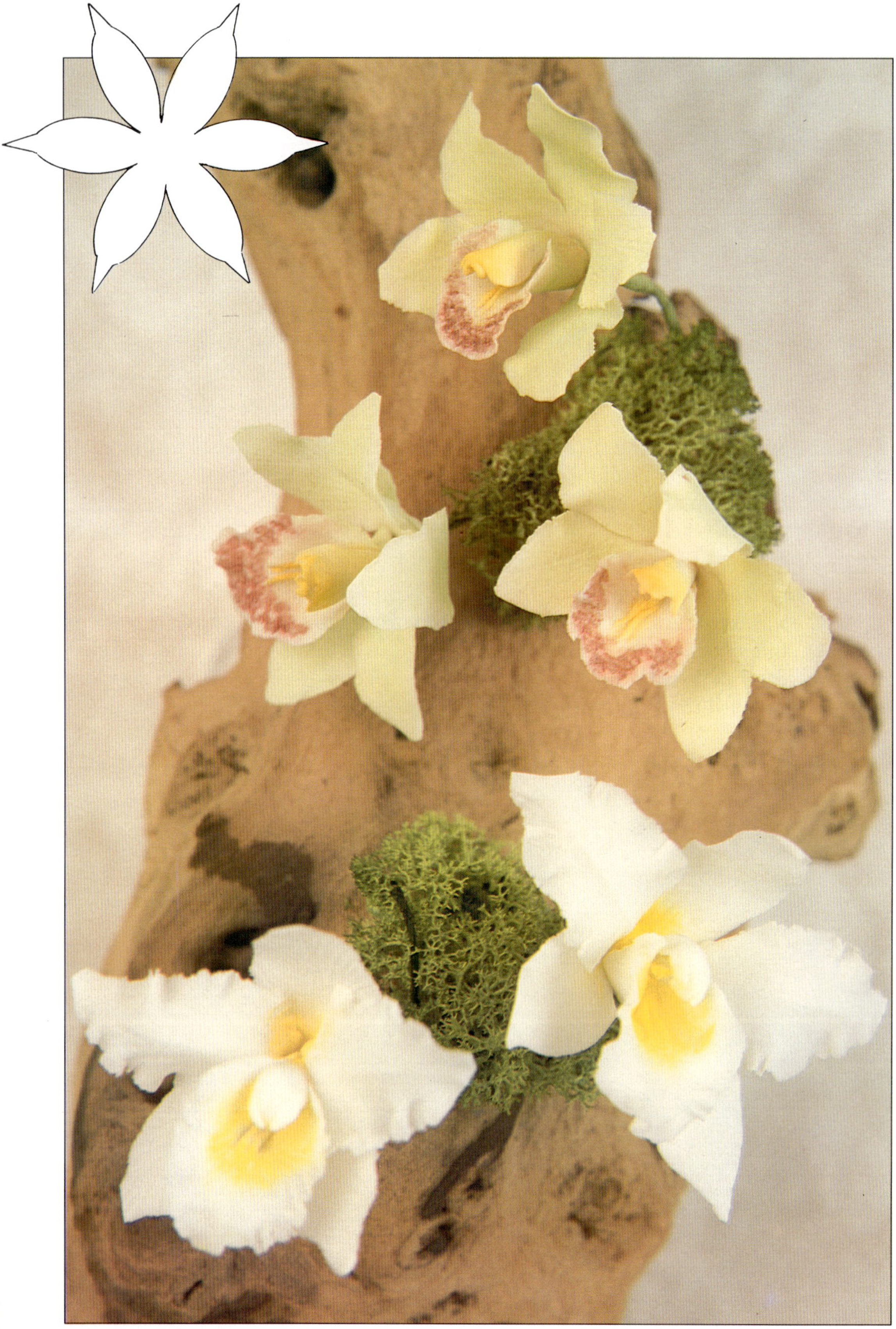

SOME MORE FLOWERS TO TRY:
DAFFODIL

The centre and trumpet
Tape six short yellow stamens onto a 26g wire. To make the trumpet roll out a piece of yellow paste thinly and cut a piece 1¼-1½ inches long and ¾ inches wide (size given is suitable when using a 2" calyx cutter). Vein on a corn husk veiner, frill the top edge and gum down one end. Pinch together at the bottom round a small modelling stick to keep the shape. Insert the wired centre and leave to dry.

The petals
Roll a disc of yellow paste thinly over the medium hole in the pad (greased and on the coated side) to form a shallow mexican hat. Turn out onto a board and cut out the petals using a six sepal calyx cutter. Snip between the petals.

Place on the foam surface of the pad and thin and vein three alternate petals. Bring these forward to become the inner petal layer and lift out of the way of the others. Thin and vein the remaining three petals. Open up the flower centre with a modelling stick and push the wired centre into position, moulding the paste at the back to the wire. Support with sponge if necessary.

Stage 4
Push a small ball of green paste into position at the back of the flower. Roll out some straw/beige coloured paste and cut out a teardrop shape to make the sheath. Buds can be made from cones of yellow and green paste, and some flowers should be made with petals partly closed. The leaves can be cut by hand (see template on page 47) and should be veined and dried before dusting.

TULIP

The flower centre

Make a hook on the end of a 24g wire. Take a ball of yellow/green paste (colour varies with variety of tulip) and work into a sausage shape on the wire to represent the pistil. Pinch at the top to make three ridges and leave to dry. Tape three folded stamens (six heads) around the pistil.

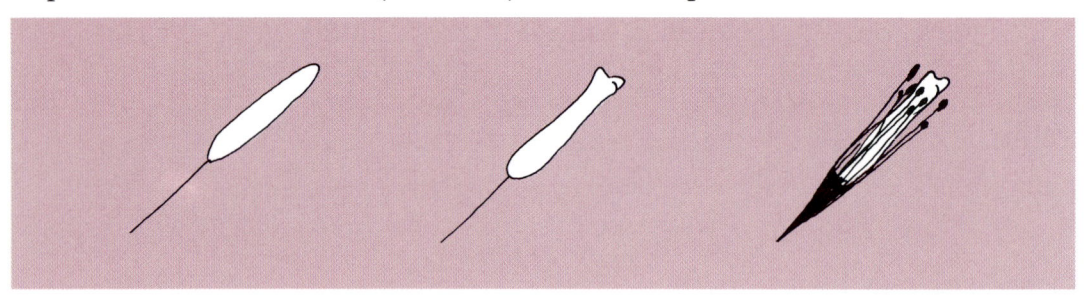

The petals

Roll out a piece of paste on the coated and greased side of the pad to create a mexican hat with a tiny shallow bump. Remove and cut petals with a six petalled blossom cutter. Place the petals on the other side of the pad and stretch and vein them - three to become the inner petals and three the outer.

Flower assembly

Gum round the pistil base and push the wire down through the centre of the petals. Place in a deep foam former as shown below. Check that the petals are evenly spaced and separate with foam chips if desired. When completely dry, remove from former and dust - some tulips are yellow around the base of the pistil and others black.

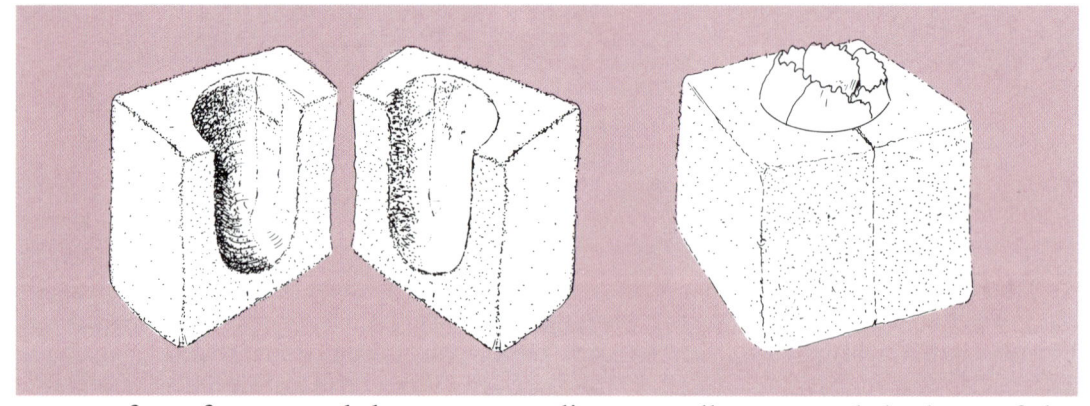

The leaves

Leaves can be cut freehand and should be veined with a veining tool before being left to dry in a variety of curved and curled shapes. When completely dry, they should be dusted - some can be very dark in colour and some black added to green powder should help to achieve the correct colouring.

37

CYCLAMEN

The flower back

The flower back is made from a cone of paste coloured to match the flower colour. Form a small cup and place on the end of a 'T' bar hooked 26g wire. Add a small calyx, and bend the wire into an 'S' shape.

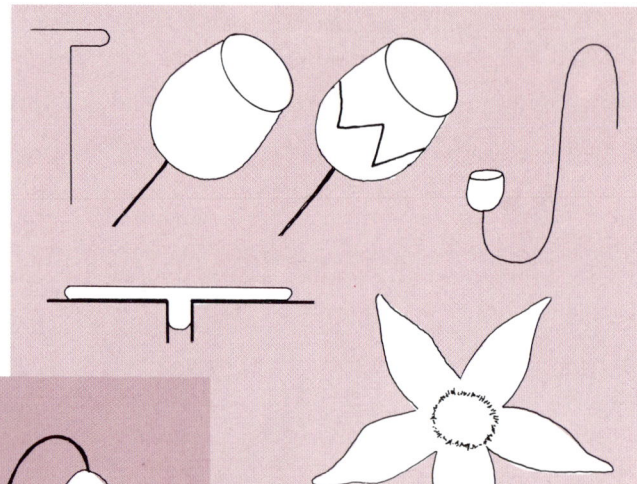

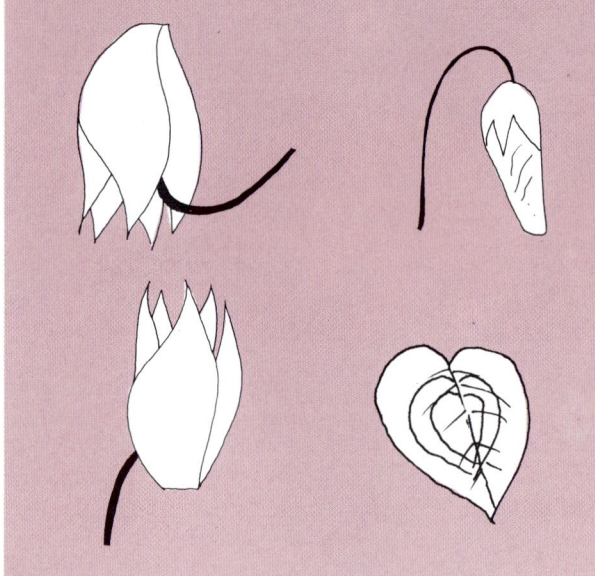

The petals

Place a disc of paste over the medium hole in the pad and roll thinly (use other holes for different sizes). This will create a shallow mexican hat on the back. Remove and place it on a board and cut out petals with a large five sepalled calyx cutter. If you only have a six sepal calyx, use it and cut away one sepal.

Snip between the petals, and thin and shape them on the foam surface of the pad. Vein on a husk veiner - take care to vein each petal from the centre and lightly curve the petal centres with a ball tool as if marking a central vein. Brush the inside of the dried cup with gum as well as the outside between the calyx points. Place the shallow centre into the cup and allow the petals to hang down. Pinch the petals round the rim of the cup and hollow out the centre with a modelling stick. Dry with the petals hanging upside down.

The buds and leaves

When dry, dust the bottom of the petals and inside the flower mouth with darker colouring. Make the buds from a cone of coloured paste, and cut with scissors to represent the petals. Twist to give characteristic shape and add a calyx. The leaves are heart-shaped, but without a sharp point and can be cut out by hand with scissors, (or cut round a template with a sharp knife). Bend a wire at right angles before inserting into the leaf and, when dry, dust a fairly dark green colour. Paint white markings on the front and brush the backs with a pinkish colour before passing through steam. The flower, bud and leaf stems should be pinkish in colour and should be lightly dusted with a mixture of pink and brown.

USING CELPOTS

CelPots provide an ideal method of arranging sugar flowers based on a special cutter, a plastic container and a foam insert (a perspex holder can also be used for display). The flowers can be placed near to the cake surface without it being pierced, and are arranged in the foam in a similar manner to real flowers in florist's foam.

Stage 1

Preferably straight after covering (or within two days and whilst the icing is still soft) a cake with sugarpaste (CelPots can also be used with royal icing), cut a cavity in the cake by placing the CelPot cutter on the cake surface where you want the flower arrangement to be positioned. If you think the cake might crumble, prepare a paper mask with a hole in it and lay over the cake surface. Twist to cut through the icing and then push down into the cake for about 1 inch. Twist again, so that the wire inside the cutter cuts through the cake (like an apple corer) and then lift out to create a hole. Remove the cake from the cutter and wash.

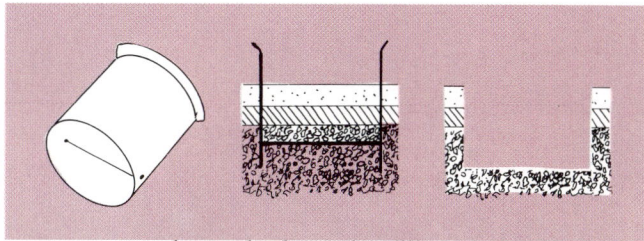

Stage 2

If desired, cut out a disc of marzipan with the cutter and place in the bottom of the cavity. Cover the inverted CelPot with sugarpaste (about G inch thick) and trim away excess paste with the top rim of the cutter (take care with the sharp cutter edge!) Invert the pot into the hole in the cake and then remove, leaving the sugarpaste in the cake. Press together at the joins in the paste and smooth over the cake surface with a smoother.

IMPORTANT NOTE:

Do not use cornflour (cornstarch) when rolling out sugarpaste to stop it sticking to the pot etc. Cornflour which comes into contact with almond paste can cause fermentation!

Stage 3

Push the foam firmly into the CelPot. The foam is intentionally deeper than the plastic container so that flowers and leaves can be inserted at the side, low to the cake surface. Dust the foam surface with colouring if desired. The method for arranging sugar flowers is similar to that used with real flowers in florist's foam. For fine wire stems, first make a hole with a fine pointed modelling tool or cocktail stick before pressing wire into place. Tweezers should be used to grip wires (near the bottom of the wire will allow better control and pressure). When the arrangement is complete, place the CelPot in the prepared cavity in the cake. After the celebration, the CelPot can be placed in a holder for display.

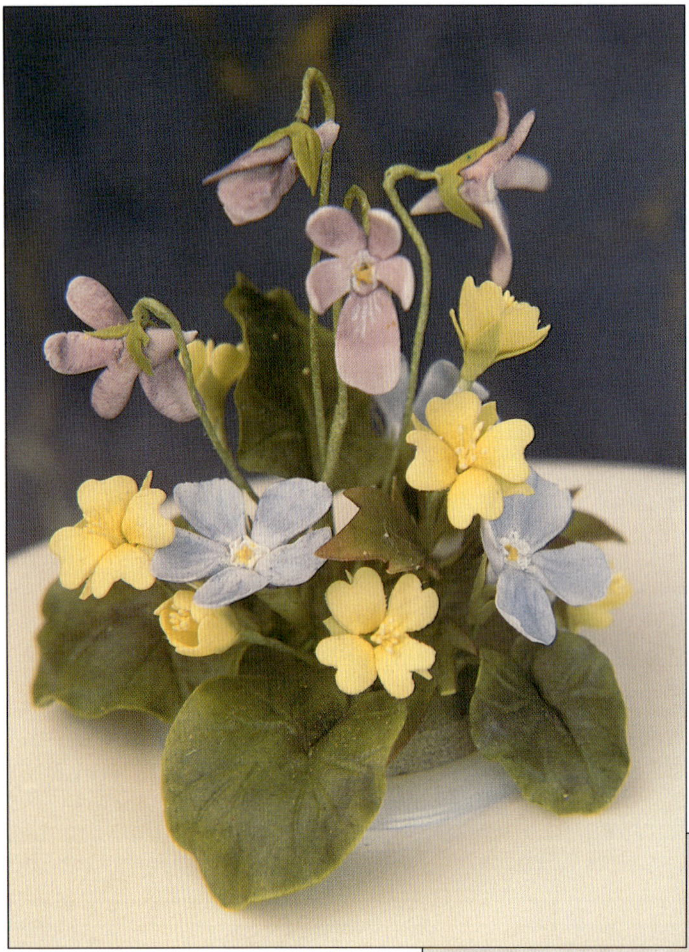

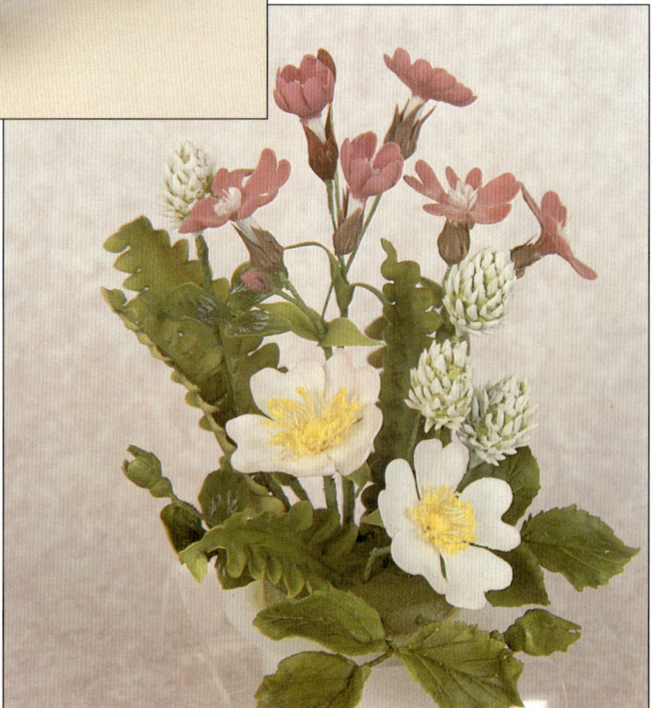

NATURAL (Growing) and RANDOM Settings

This type of arrangement is particularly well suited to wild flowers or those that do not readily combine with other flowers (e.g. anemones). The following points should guide you to a successful arrangement.

- colour combinations should give the spray enough vitality to attract attention, whilst maintaining balance
- the flower selection should include those flowers seen at a particular time of year, and normally from the same habitat
- at least one variety should have broad leaves, to give good cover and a firm base to the arrangement
- flowers and leaves of different shape make more interesting combinations

Stage 1 Add leaf cover for the pot surface and background foliage.

Stage 2 Fill the sides and top of the arrangement with interesting variation in colour and shape - perhaps taller spiky flowers and leaves.

Stage 3 Add the focal detail, which should stand slightly forward of the background.

BOUQUET Setting

Used mainly for wedding and celebration cake decoration, and often tightly compact and combined with an extended and pointed spray. Usually limited to those fairly robust flowers that can be arranged close to each other. Delicate blooms (e.g. daisies) can easily be damaged, but the advantage of arranging in a CelPot, is that it is easy to replace a flower without disturbing the others!

Stage 1 Wire a pointed spray by taping small blossoms and filler flowers together. Make a bend in the handle so that it can be pushed into the foam. Secure with wire staples made from short lengths of 24g wire, to hold the stem firmly in position.

Stage 2 Decide upon where the arrangement will be viewed from and add flowers and leaves to the background, including using the sides of the foam to achieve good cover of flowers next to the cake surface.

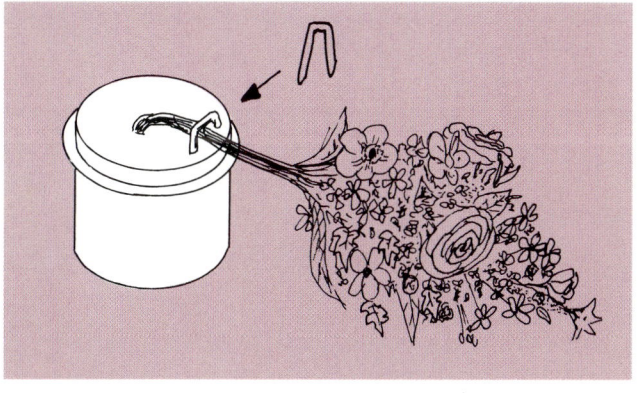

Stage 3 Add eye-catching flowers to the front to give the bouquet a dramatic focus.

TRIANGULAR *setting*

In a similar way to the bouquet spray, the triangular spray has extensions - one to the top, and two to the bottom corners. The setting is particularly effective, and more interesting as a cake decoration, if sloped backwards from the viewpoint.

Stage 1 Assemble and position the three pointed sprays as shown - wire staples will only be needed for larger sprays. The lower sprays should come forward and the top spray should lean back.

Stage 2 Fill the sides with more rounded shapes and arrange good cover at the front.

Stage 3 Add flowers and leaves to the focal area, using a variety of shapes and colours to dramatic effect.

43

LEAVES

Remember that flowers are rarely seen without leaves, and that leaves are a vital part of any arrangement. By selecting interesting leaf shapes, colours and textures (patterning and veining etc.) the arrangement can be greatly enhanced. The triangular setting on the last page serves as an example of how effective leaves can be - even when on their own! A foliage spray can be a very appropriate decoration for a man's cake.

SPECIMEN Settings

One major advantage over the traditional methods of setting sugar flowers, is that the CelPot offers more scope for variation in spray design. It is possible to make an arrangement that fits the character of the plant or flower. An example can be seen in the cyclamen which is arranged as if in a plant pot - the way that we are used to seeing this particular plant. Some plants display a particular erect, trailing or hanging habit, and as an example, the fuchsia could be arranged hanging over a lower posy of small flowers. In the diagrammatic representation, small pointed sprays are arched into a swirl, giving the whole setting a sense of movement.

POSY Settings

Cake decorations are often low and fairly compact and CelPots are ideal for creating these cushion-like arrangements. One of the major advantages with a CelPot is that it is so easy to re-arrange a spray. Flowers and leaves can easily be replaced or exchanged without disturbing the main spray.

Stage 1 Base the cushion outline on a geometric shape and position the outer sprays (diamond example).

Stage 2 Fill the sides with small flowers and leaf cover.

Stage 3 Add the main flowers in the central focal area.

45

CUTTER TEMPLATES 3", 2½", 2" & 1½"

FIVE PETALLED BLOSSOM CUTTERS

SIX PETALLED BLOSSOM CUTTERS

FIVE POINTED CALYX CUTTERS

SIX POINTED CALYX CUTTERS

LEAF TEMPLATES

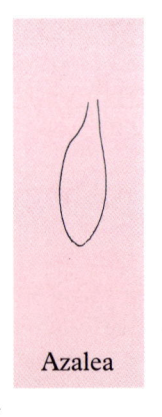

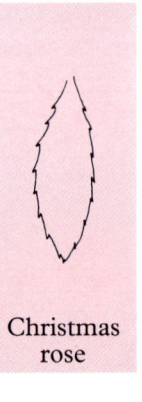

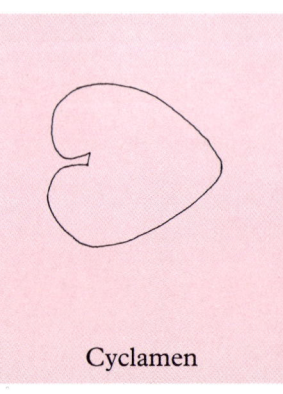

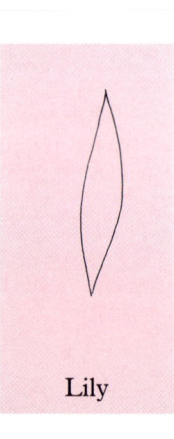

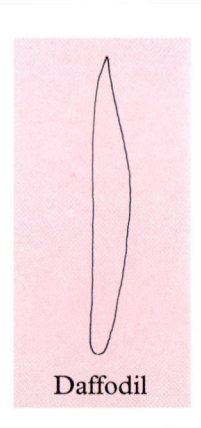

| Azalea | Christmas rose | Cyclamen | Lily | Daffodil |

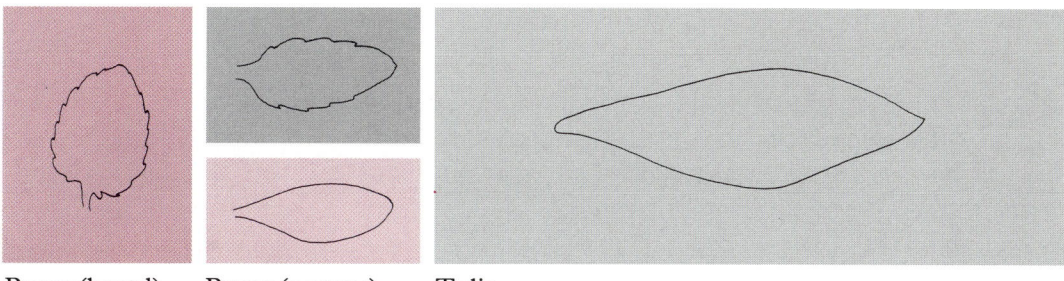

Pansy (broad) Pansy (narrow) Tulip
                Sweet Pea

PASTE RECIPE

Flower Modelling paste (Gumpaste)

There are many different recipes for flower modelling paste, including excellent ones to be found in the following books:

The Int. School of Sugarcraft Bk2 Nicholas Lodge Merehurst ISBN 0 948075 78 3

Finishing Touches Tombi Peck & Pat Ashby Merehurst ISBN 0 948075 03 1

A similar recipe, which I use, requires the use of a heavy duty mixer, and the method is given below:

Ingred. 1 lb (485 grm) sieved powdered sugar
        3 teasp. (15ml) gum tragacanth
        5 teasp. (25ml) cold water
        2 teasp. (10ml) powdered gelatine
        3 teasp. (15ml) shortening or white fat
        2 teasp. (10ml) liquid glucose
        7 teasp. (35ml) reconstituted dried albumen

Sieve the powdered sugar and the gum tragacanth into an ovenproof bowl and place in a cool oven (100 deg.C) for about 20 minutes. The sugar should be warm to the touch.

Place the water in a heatproof jug, sprinkle in the gelatine, and leave to soak. Stand in a pan of water over a low heat, and stir until clear (and thoroughly dissolved, to avoid sandy texture later). DO NOT BOIL. Add the white fat and liquid glucose and heat gently until all the three ingredients are liquified. Remove the sugar and gum from the oven, add the dissolved liquid and the albumen, blending with a wooden spoon. (At this stage, speed is important as the mixture cools very quickly.) Insert the bowl into the mixer with flat ('K') beater fitted, and mix for approx. 5 minutes at the lowest speed. The grey slushy mixture should become white and 'stringy.' Insufficient beating will result in an off-white coloured paste which is too soft - the mixture should be gummy and stringy, but snow-white and firm to the touch. (DO NOT leave mixer unattended whilst beating, since the mixture becomes very stiff - it is a good idea to press down on the mixer arm to prevent or reduce strain on the motor.)

Put the mixture in a clean airtight plastic bag, squeezing out any air, and leave to cool. When cold, place in an airtight container in the refrigerator for 24 hours before using.

The paste will set quite firm and when required, lightly grease your hands with some white fat and thoroughly knead a piece the size of a golf ball until it is soft, elastic and pliable. If too dry, add a small amount of fat, and if crumbly, some liquid albumen. Remember that fat slows down the drying process, whilst extra albumen makes the paste more pliable. The paste should always be stored in a refrigerator and will keep for 6-8 weeks. The paste is also suitable for freezing.

GUM OR GLUE?

The use of the term "gum" in the text refers to either egg white or gum arabic. A very good "glue" for sticking dried pieces together (e.g. repairing broken petals) is made by mixing a small amount of flower modelling paste with egg white to make a thick sticky substance.

THE AUTHOR

Margaret Ford, who trained at the Robert Gordon College in Aberdeen, has a reputation for high standards in sugarcraft technique and teaching methods. In recent years she has successfully combined this with the development of the "CelCakes" range of sugar-craft equipment. Margaret has made four trips to the U.S.A. to demonstrate and teach. She regularly demonstrates at British Sugarcraft Guild meetings.

Margaret has also worked with other internationally known experts in sugarcraft on the Sugarcraft Roadshow, and her publications include *Blooming Quick*, *Designs On Wiring* and *Designs On Foliage*.

ACKNOWLEDGEMENT

Our thanks to Sally Harris (Tinkertech Two) for the development of special cutters.

CELFORMERS

CelFormers are made from polystyrene and are ideal for supporting sugar flowers and leaves when left to dry. There are two shapes (each in three different sizes) – one for cupped flowers and the other for the support of inner and outer petals (e.g. lilies).

If the florists wire is pushed through the former and secured with a paper clip under the former, the wire can be pushed into a foam block for drying (or bent at right angles and left on a flat surface during drying).